CYPRUS THROUGH THE AGES

A BRIEF HISTORY

By

Martin Miller-Yianni

COPYRIGHT AND ACKNOWLEDGEMENTS

Publisher: Martin Miller-Yianni, Yambol, Bulgaria

First Printed Edition 2023

ISBN 978-619-7742-23-7 (ePub)

ISBN 978-619-7742-22-0 (Paperback)

A CIP catalogue record for this book is available from:

The National Register of Published Books in Bulgaria

bulevard 'Vasil Levski' 88,

1504 Sofia,

Bulgaria

Cover Photograph – Kykkos Monastery

By Athina Vrikki from unsplash.com

All Internal photographs and images are courtesy of Wikipedia

TABLE OF CONTENTS

INTRODUCTION

Whether you're a student, an inquisitive traveller, or someone keen to explore Cyprus' history, "Cyprus Through the Ages: A Brief History" is an invaluable resource. As part of a broader series on the histories of various countries, this book is well-organised and clearly presented, facilitating easy navigation through different historical periods and chapters, allowing readers to swiftly find specific information.

From Cyprus' ancient civilisations to its modern developments, this book thoroughly covers the key aspects of the island's history. It enables readers to understand the historical context and cultural heritage of Cyprus. Its concise format makes it an ideal choice for those seeking a quick reference or an introduction to the island's past.

This book offers a thorough overview without sacrificing accuracy or depth. It presents information in a readable and accessible British English style, making it an excellent resource for gaining insight into Cyprus' diverse historical foundations.

It's worth noting that some chapters may seem to revisit important events. This is unavoidable as transitional eras often share events and significant figures, helping to reinforce the interconnectedness of Cyprus' history. Such recapitulations act as valuable reminders, aiding in the understanding of the broader historical narrative.

Whether you wish to refresh your knowledge of a specific era or develop a general understanding of Cyprus' past, the book provides reliable information and serves as an invaluable guide. It immerses readers in the triumphs, challenges, and cultural transformations that have shaped Cyprus' identity, offering a fascinating journey through time.

"Cyprus Through the Ages: A Brief History" is an engaging and informative book that provides a concise yet thorough look at Cyprus' history. It is an exceptional resource for anyone eager to explore the captivating story of this Mediterranean island and gain a deeper appreciation for its rich cultural heritage.

The Flag of Cyprus

The flag of Cyprus, adopted on August 16, 1960, features a white field with a copper-orange silhouette of the island in the centre. Two olive branches, symbolising peace, cross underneath the island. The white background represents the purity and peace of the island, while the copper-orange colour represents the rich copper deposits that have historically been significant for Cyprus. The map of the island and the olive branches are symbols of unity and hope for peaceful coexistence between the Greek Cypriot and Turkish Cypriot communities on the island, despite the ongoing division of Cyprus.

Cyprus's Location

Cyprus is a strategically positioned island nation in the Eastern Mediterranean, located approximately between latitudes 34° and 36° North and longitudes 32° and 35° East. It lies just south of the southern coast of Turkey, with its closest point to the Turkish mainland about 40 miles (64 kilometres) away. To the west, it is in proximity to the southern coast of Greece. Cyprus is the third-largest Mediterranean island and boasts a diverse landscape, including mountains, coastal plains, and a central mesa. Its Mediterranean climate, featuring hot, dry summers and mild, wet winters, has made it an attractive destination. Cyprus has been divided since 1974, with the Republic of Cyprus controlling the southern two-thirds and the Turkish Republic of Northern Cyprus (recognised only by Turkey) occupying the northern third, separated by the "Green Line, " or "Buffer Zone. "

Cyprus, a land steeped in the annals of history, stands as an enduring testament to humanity's timeless journey through the corridors of time. Its rich embedment of history, spanning millennia, weaves a captivating narrative interlaced with the threads of culture, conquest, and civilisation. From its earliest inhabitants to the height of Hellenistic rule, Cyprus's historical voyage unfolds as a mesmerising epic, leaving an indelible imprint on the scrolls of antiquity.

THE DAWN OF CIVILISATION

Around 10,000 B.C., intrepid souls embarked upon a voyage into the fertile lands of the Eastern Mediterranean, where Cyprus, with its clement climate and abundant natural resources, provided a nurturing place for budding communities. These early Cypriots, celebrated for their resourcefulness, relied on hunting, gathering, and rudimentary agriculture.

The earliest confirmed traces of human activity in Cyprus date back to Aetokremnos, nestled along the island's southern coast, around 10,000 B.C. Settlements began to emerge by 8200 B.C., coinciding with the extinction of the Cyprus dwarf hippopotamus and elephant. Astonishingly, ancient water wells, estimated to be between 9,000 and 10,500 years old, have been unearthed.

Fossils at Aetokremnos

At a Neolithic site on Cyprus, archaeologists unearthed the remains of an 8-month-old cat interred alongside a human body, dating back approximately 9,500 years. This predates the ancient Egyptian civilisation and signifies an early connection between humans and felines. The exquisitely preserved Neolithic village of Khirokitia, founded around 6800 B.C., proudly boasts its UNESCO World Heritage Site status.

The Site of Khirokitia

Around 1200 B.C., Cyprus bore witness to the emergence of distinct city-states, each with its own unique character and cultural identity. Kition, heavily influenced by the Phoenicians, assumed a vital role in Cyprus's commercial and maritime development, nurturing trade networks that spanned the breadth of the Mediterranean.

Ancient City of Kition

To the west, Paphos garnered renowned for its association with Aphrodite the Greek goddess of love and beauty. It evolved into a revered centre of religious pilgrimage, drawing devotees from far-flung lands.

This era marked a dynamic convergence of cultures, beliefs, and economic activities in Cyprus. City-states like Kition and Paphos served as veritable crucibles of cultural fusion.

Aphrodite - The Goddess of Love

In 525 B.C., Cyprus fell under the dominion of the Persians, experiencing both prosperity and cultural exchanges within the vast trade network of the Persian Empire. However, foreign rule bred discontent.

In 333 B.C., the mighty Alexander the Great and his Hellenistic successors asserted their control over Cyprus, inaugurating an age of profound Greek influence and Hellenisation. Greek culture thrived, imprinting its essence on every facet of life on the island.

Prominent locales and figures from this time included Paphos, Salamis, Kourion, Soli, and the philosopher Philokypros. The enduring legacy of this Hellenistic era still resonates in Cyprus's language, art, and architecture to this very day.

IMPORTANT PLACES:

Aetokremnos: An archaeological site along Cyprus's southern coast, dating back to around 10,000 B.C., offering insights into early human activity.

Khirokitia: An exceptionally well-preserved Neolithic village founded around 6800 B.C., designated as a UNESCO World Heritage Site.

Kition: An ancient city-state heavily influenced by the Phoenicians, playing a pivotal role in Cyprus's commercial and maritime development.

Paphos: Known for its association with Aphrodite the Greek goddess of love and beauty, becoming a revered centre of religious pilgrimage.

Salamis: An ancient city on Cyprus's east coast, with a rich history dating back to the Bronze Age, playing a crucial role in the Hellenistic period.

Kourion: An ancient city located on the southern coast, boasting remarkable archaeological remains, including a well-preserved Roman amphitheatre.

Soli: An ancient city on the north coast of Cyprus, which thrived during the Hellenistic era.

In the wake of Alexander the Great's conquest of Cyprus in 333 B.C., the island embarked on a transformative journey that forever altered its historical course. This pivotal period ushered in a new chapter in Cyprus's narrative, one deeply entwined with Hellenistic culture, setting the stage for the era of Roman dominion.

ALEXANDER'S ARRIVAL AND THE INFLUX OF HELLENISTIC INFLUENCE

Alexander's swift and decisive arrival on Cyprus signified a momentous juncture in its history. With his conquest came an integration into the Hellenistic world, and the Greek imprint began to permeate every facet of Cypriot life. This transformation commenced with the adoption of the Greek language, a linguistic shift that facilitated communication and bound Cyprus closer to Greek literature and philosophy.

The profound impact of Hellenistic culture extended to the realm of art and architecture. Greek artistic styles, including the distinguished Doric, Ionic, and Corinthian orders, became prominent in construction. Cypriot artisans enthusiastically embraced Hellenistic aesthetics, imbuing their creations with a Greek artistic flair.

Alexander The Great (Mosaic)

The intellectual landscape of Cyprus also underwent a profound transformation, with schools of thought influenced by eminent figures like Aristotle and Plato flourishing. These institutions contributed to the development of an educated elite class, fostering a culture of intellectual enlightenment.

Head of Aristotle

Bust of Plato

In this era, Cyprus flourished as vibrant hubs of culture, learning, and commerce. These city-states emerged as centres of intellectual exchange, catalysing the emergence of a distinctive Cypriot intellectual and artistic identity.

Paphos, in particular, remained a sanctuary consecrated to the goddess Aphrodite, attracting pilgrims and devotees from across the Mediterranean. Here, the unique fusion of local beliefs and Greek mythology was beautifully exemplified, showcasing the island's singular cultural blend.

Cyprus's experience under Hellenistic influence was characterised by cultural dynamism, an effervescent intellectual atmosphere, and the harmonious blending of age-old traditions.

TRANSITION TO ROMAN RULE: A NEW ERA

The year 58 B.C. heralded a significant shift in the political landscape of Cyprus as the Roman Republic assumed control. This transition ushered in an era of remarkable engineering feats and transformation of the island's terrain.

Romans, known for their engineering prowess, left an indelible mark on Cyprus's landscape. An intricate network of roads, bridges, and aqueducts crisscrossed the island, bearing testimony to Roman innovation.

Roman Aqueduct in Nicosia

These Roman-engineered marvels did not merely serve practical purposes. They added to the island's grandeur, demonstrating the Romans' dedication to modernising the regions under their rule.

THRIVING UNDER PAX ROMANA

Cyprus thrived under the umbrella of Pax Romana, a time characterised by relative peace and stability across the vast Roman Empire. The island's strategic location in the Roman trade network was a boon, its ports bustling with activity and serving as crucibles of commerce and cultural exchange.

The extensive infrastructure development not only improved transportation and communication but also underscored the Romans' commitment to elevating the island's status.

Political stability, efficient governance, and the Roman military presence ensured security, shielding Cyprus from external threats. This era of prosperity elevated living standards and bequeathed a profound Roman influence upon Cyprus's culture, society, and governance.

AGRICULTURAL ABUNDANCE AND THE WINE TRADE

Cyprus's fertile soils and temperate climate yielded bountiful agricultural harvests. The cultivation of grains, olives, and fruits not only sustained the population but also contributed to the broader Mediterranean food supply.

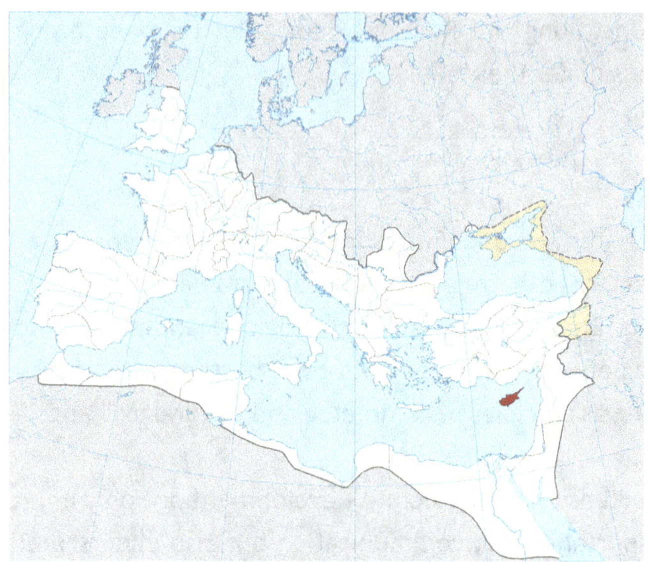

The Roman Empire 125 A.D.

Yet, it was in the realm of viticulture that Cyprus truly shone. The island's vineyards and winemaking flourished, producing wines of exceptional quality. These wines, highly esteemed, were not merely commodities for export but symbols of hospitality and conviviality, intertwined with celebrations, religious rituals, and social gatherings.

STRATEGIC SIGNIFICANCE AND TRADE HUB

Cyprus's strategic placement in the Eastern Mediterranean made it a linchpin in Rome's expansive trade network. Its ports assumed a pivotal role in maritime trade, facilitating commerce and the exchange of cultures.

The island's role as a nexus of trade bolstered its economic significance, allowing it to flourish both economically and culturally, as it thrived on the trade flowing through its ports.

CYPRUS: A SANCTUARY FOR PROMINENT EXILES

Notably, Cyprus garnered a reputation as a refuge for prominent figures from Roman politics and society who had fallen out of favour. Among them was the philosopher and statesman Seneca, who sought asylum on the island during his exile.

Seneca's presence on Cyprus offered a unique perspective into its character, culture, and philosophical musings. His writings from his time in exile provide invaluable glimpses into Cyprus's landscape, its people, and their way of life. Seneca's sojourn on the island likely contributed to the flourishing intellectual and cultural milieu, fostering the exchange of ideas and the pursuit of intellectual endeavours.

THE ENDURING LEGACY

As we contemplate Cyprus's journey through the Hellenistic and Roman rules, we discern a profound and enduring legacy that continues to shape the modern island. The cultural heritage of Cyprus, deeply rooted in Hellenistic traditions and enriched by Roman innovations, has left an indelible mark on its identity.

The remnants of grand Roman villas, ancient temples, and echoes of philosophical wisdom serve as enduring testaments to the island's extraordinary trek through time. As we delve deeper into Cyprus's history, we do so with an appreciation for the enduring spirit that has been passed down through the ages.

Emperor Nero and Seneca

Alexander the Great: Alexander's conquest of Cyprus marked the beginning of the island's transformation. His military leadership and vision led to the integration of Cyprus into the Hellenistic world.

Aristotle and Plato: The intellectual landscape of Cyprus was greatly influenced by the teachings of these renowned philosophers, whose ideas thrived in schools of thought on the island.

Seneca: The philosopher and statesman found refuge on Cyprus during his exile. His writings offer insights into the island's culture and intellectual life during Roman rule.

IMPORTANT PLACES:

Paphos: Paphos was a significant cultural and religious centre. It remained dedicated to the goddess Aphrodite and showcased a unique blend of local beliefs and Greek mythology.

Cyprus City-States: Various city-states on Cyprus, such as Salamis, Kourion, and Soli, emerged as hubs of culture, learning, and commerce during this period.

Roman Infrastructure: The extensive network of roads, bridges, and aqueducts constructed by the Romans played a crucial role in transforming the island's landscape and facilitating trade and communication.

Cyprus Ports: The ports of Cyprus, including those in Paphos and Salamis, were vital to the island's role as a trade hub in the Eastern Mediterranean, connecting it to the broader Roman world.

The Byzantine era, spanning from 330 A.D. to 1191 A.D., stands as a dynamic and transformative chapter in the history of Cyprus. This period is characterised by several pivotal aspects that left an influential mark on the island's identity and cultural heritage.

A BEACON OF BYZANTINE CHRISTIANITY

Foremost among these aspects is the enduring religious influence that defined Byzantine Cyprus. During this time, Cyprus became a bastion of Byzantine Christianity, witnessing the widespread adoption of the faith, the construction of numerous churches and monasteries, and the emergence of a robust religious hierarchy. This religious transformation had a profound and enduring impact, shaping the spirituality, religious practices, and cultural traditions of the island.

The Byzantine era was not without its share of political upheavals. Cyprus saw changes in governance and rulership, with various Byzantine emperors and administrators asserting their authority at different times. External threats and invasions further added to the island's political complexities, leaving an indelible mark on its history and its relationship with the broader Byzantine Empire.

Amid these political and religious changes, Cyprus displayed remarkable cultural resilience. The island continued to produce distinctive works of art, including Byzantine-style religious icons, mosaics, and manuscripts. These cultural achievements attest to Cyprus's ability to preserve its artistic heritage while adapting to the evolving cultural landscape of the Byzantine world.

A Typical Byzantine Religious Icon

The Byzantine era was a transformative period for Cyprus, as it evolved from its ancient and Hellenistic roots into a stronghold of Byzantine Christianity. This transformation significantly influenced the island's identity, aligning it more closely with the religious and cultural heritage of the Byzantine Empire.

In the year 330 A.D., Cyprus's destiny took a momentous turn as it was integrated into the Byzantine Empire under the enlightened rule of Emperor Constantine the Great. This historic integration marked the beginning of a profound transformation for the island, with far-reaching implications that would shape its identity for centuries to come.

Emperor Constantine the Great, celebrated for his pivotal role in the history of the Roman Empire, brought about this integration. Notably, he is known for embracing Christianity and promoting religious tolerance. Under his enlightened rule, Cyprus became an integral part of the Byzantine Empire, both politically and culturally.

Constantine the Great

Cyprus's strategic location in the Eastern Mediterranean positioned it as a crucial ecclesiastical centre within the Byzantine Empire. The island played a pivotal role in facilitating the exchange of religious ideas and practices between the empire and the Holy Land. Bishops and archbishops on the island wielded significant influence, shaping the religious affairs of the Byzantine Empire and underscoring Cyprus's importance in the Eastern Christian world.

The Archbishop of Cyprus held a prestigious and influential position within the Byzantine religious hierarchy. This office wielded substantial religious and political authority, further elevating the island's significance in the Byzantine religious landscape.

Saint Barnabas, a prominent figure during this era, is traditionally regarded as the founder of the Cypriot Orthodox Church. His role in spreading Christianity across the island and his significance in the early Christian community left an indelible mark on Cyprus's religious landscape. The enduring reverence for Saint Barnabas underscores the island's deep Christian roots.

Saint Barnabas

The passion for religion during the Byzantine era led to the construction of numerous monasteries and churches across Cyprus. Many of these edifices still stand today as awe-inspiring architectural wonders, bearing witness to the exceptional craftsmanship and devotion of the time. Notable examples include the Kykkos Monastery and the Church of Panagia Angeloktisti in Kiti, which serve as remarkable testaments to Byzantine art and architecture.

CHALLENGES AND THE CRUSADER INTERLUDE

However, the Byzantine era was not without its challenges. In the late 11th century, Cyprus faced raids by Muslim forces from the east, causing instability and uncertainty. These raids disrupted the island's relatively peaceful existence and highlighted its vulnerability to external threats.

In 1191, Cyprus found itself at a significant crossroads in history when Richard the Lionheart of England, a prominent figure of the Third Crusade, conquered the island. Richard's arrival and brief but impactful rule left a lasting mark on Cyprus's history, even though the island remained under nominal Byzantine control.

Richard the Lionheart, known for his military prowess and participation in the Crusades, brought about a period of notable change during his rule of Cyprus. His administration introduced elements of Norman governance and culture to the island, including the establishment of feudal practices and the construction of Norman-style castles and fortifications. Some of these structures still stand today as historical landmarks.

Despite these changes, Cyprus remained under nominal Byzantine control during Richard's rule, reflecting the island's complex political status and the various influences it experienced.

LEGACY OF BYZANTINE CYPRUS

The Byzantine era's enduring legacy is palpable in modern Cyprus. It forged a profound and enduring connection between the island and the Greek Orthodox Church, shaping cultural traditions, festivals, and religious practices deeply rooted in its Byzantine heritage.

Cyprus's rich cultural and religious heritage, anchored in its connection to the Greek Orthodox Church, is a defining feature of its identity. The Byzantine period left an indelible mark on the island, evident in its Orthodox traditions and the veneration of saints, many of whom lived during that era.

The era was also prolific for the creation of exquisite religious art, including icons, mosaics, and religious manuscripts. These artistic treasures, born from deep spiritual devotion and artistic richness, continue to be revered as priceless cultural and religious assets, offering a tangible link to the vibrant artistic tradition of Byzantine Cyprus.

Cyprus's history during the Byzantine era showcases its remarkable resilience and capacity to absorb diverse influences while preserving its unique identity. This period serves as a cornerstone of Cyprus's identity, reflecting its ability to adapt, evolve, and preserve its cultural and religious heritage in the face of changing times.

INFLUENTIAL FIGURES:

Emperor Constantine the Great: As the Byzantine Emperor responsible for Cyprus's integration into the Byzantine Empire in 330 A.D., he played a pivotal role in shaping the Island's destiny and religious landscape.

Saint Barnabas: A prominent figure during this era, Saint Barnabas is traditionally regarded as the founder of the Cypriot Orthodox Church. His efforts in spreading Christianity across the island left a lasting impact on Cyprus's religious identity.

Richard the Lionheart: Although not a Byzantine figure, Richard's conquest of Cyprus in 1191 A.D. marked a significant turning point in the island's history. His rule introduced Norman influences and changes to governance and fortifications.

Cyprus Monasteries and Churches: During the Byzantine era, numerous monasteries and churches were constructed across Cyprus. Notable examples include:
  - **Kykkos Monastery**: An important religious site known for its stunning architecture and religious significance.
  - **Church of Panagia Angeloktisti in Kiti**: Renowned for its Byzantine art and architecture, it showcases the artistic achievements of the time.

Cyprus Castles and Fortifications: The Norman-style castles and fortifications built during Richard the Lionheart's rule are historically significant. These include:
  - **Kolossi Castle**: Constructed by the Knights Templar, it served both military and agricultural purposes.
  - **Limassol Castle**: A fortress with a rich history that witnessed various rulers and conquerors.

The medieval era, spanning from 1191 A.D. to 1489 A.D., weaves a captivating narrative in the history of Cyprus. This period is defined by the dominance of Crusaders, dynastic struggles, and a profound cultural amalgamation, creating a time of significant transformation for the island.

THE ARRIVAL OF THE CRUSADERS AND RICHARD THE LIONHEART

In the year 1191 A.D., a momentous event unfolded during the Third Crusade, altering the course of Cyprus's history. Richard the Lionheart of England, a prominent figure in the Crusades, landed in Cyprus, heralding a new era for the island. This event had far-reaching consequences, as it placed Cyprus under Crusader rule and set the stage for a complex interplay between European influence and local dynamics.

The Third Crusade, driven by European Christian forces' quest to reclaim Jerusalem from Muslim control, provided the backdrop for Richard the Lionheart's arrival in Cyprus. It marked a pivotal moment not only in the Crusades but also in Cyprus's history.

Richard's conquest of Cyprus ushered in an era of Crusader governance. His administration introduced Western European elements to the island, including feudal practices and the construction of Norman-style castles and fortifications. Despite the brevity of Richard's rule, its impact on Cyprus's political and cultural landscape was profound.

Cyprus's strategic location in the Eastern Mediterranean made it a prised possession for the Crusaders, serving as a vital logistical and resupply point for Crusader forces en route to the Holy Land. This strategic importance underscored Cyprus's enduring significance in the context of the Crusades.

Richard the Lionheart (King Richard I)

Under the Lusignan dynasty, hailing from France, Cyprus underwent a period of remarkable cultural and political transformation. This era served as a unique crucible where eastern and western traditions converged, shaping the island's identity in distinctive ways. The Lusignan monarchs, including notable figures such as Guy de Lusignan and Hugh IV, played pivotal roles in these developments. They instituted a feudal system and oversaw the construction of castles and fortifications across the island, leaving a lasting imprint. Many of these medieval fortresses, such as Kolossi Castle and St. Hilarion Castle, still stand today as enduring symbols of this remarkable era.

Guy de Lusignan

Kolossi Castle

St. Hilarion Castle

The ascent of the Lusignan dynasty to power marked a new chapter in Cyprus's history. These rulers, originating from France, introduced Western European traditions and governance, diverging from the influences of previous rulers.

One of the defining features of this period was the fusion of eastern and western traditions. Cyprus became a melting pot where these diverse cultural influences converged. This cultural amalgamation was evident in various aspects of Cypriot life, including art, architecture, cuisine, and even language.

Under Lusignan rule, Cyprus adopted a feudal system, a departure from its previous forms of governance. Feudalism brought a hierarchical structure with lords, vassals, and serfs, reshaping the island's social and political landscape.

The Lusignan Dynasty's rule in Cyprus ushered in an era of cultural fusion, political transformation, and architectural innovation. The island became a unique blend of eastern and western influences, with the feudal system and the construction of castles serving as enduring legacies of this remarkable era. Cyprus's history during the Lusignan dynasty represents a dynamic chapter in its evolution, reflecting the interplay of diverse traditions and the enduring legacy of medieval fortifications.

Cyprus during this period was characterised by the coexistence and blend of Latin, French, and Byzantine customs with its deep-rooted Byzantine heritage. This cultural synthesis was manifested in daily life, social practices, and artistic expressions, creating a distinctive and rich cultural blend that set Cyprus apart.

The Lusignan dynasty era in Cyprus was marked by the harmonious melding of Latin, French, and Byzantine cultures. This cultural synthesis was particularly evident in the island's art and architecture, where Gothic cathedrals coexisted with Byzantine churches adorned with frescoes. Cyprus's artistic diversity during this period reflected its unique position as a crossroads of cultures, resulting in a rich and enduring cultural amalgamation.

The melding of cultures had a profound impact on the island's art and architecture. Cyprus became a canvas where these diverse influences were creatively interwoven. An exemplary instance is the construction of Gothic cathedrals, such as St. Nicholas Cathedral in Famagusta. These architectural marvels bore witness to the influence of Western European design and craftsmanship.

St Nicholas Cathedral - Famagusta

Amid the introduction of Western elements, Cyprus also preserved and celebrated its Byzantine legacy. Byzantine churches adorned with intricate frescoes testified to the island's artistic diversity and creativity. These churches continued to play pivotal roles in Cyprus's spiritual and cultural life, showcasing the enduring influence of Byzantine traditions.

CHALLENGES AND OTTOMAN ENCROACHMENT

The late medieval period in Cyprus, while characterised by cultural fusion and architectural achievements, was not without its substantial trials and challenges. During this era, the island faced various external threats and conflicts that tested its resilience and stability.

Cyprus confronted incursions by the Mamluks from Egypt, posing a significant threat to the island's security. These military campaigns brought periods of instability and conflict to Cyprus as it defended itself against external forces.

Another menace during this period was the presence of Genoese pirates in the Eastern Mediterranean. These pirates disrupted maritime trade and posed a threat to Cyprus's coastal communities, contributing to a sense of insecurity and vulnerability.

Cyprus found itself embroiled in regional conflicts and rivalries, further complicating the challenges it faced. These conflicts could have economic, political, and social repercussions, making it a complex and often unsettling period for the island.

One of the most significant looming threats during this era was the expanding Ottoman Empire. The Ottomans cast a shadow over Cyprus, foreshadowing the formidable challenges that the island would face in the future. The Ottoman Empire's expansion would ultimately lead to Cyprus falling under Ottoman rule in the following centuries.

The late medieval period in Cyprus was marked by a series of trials, including Mamluk incursions, the menace of Genoese pirates, regional conflicts, and the looming presence of the expanding Ottoman Empire. These challenges tested the island's resilience and stability, setting the stage for the complex and dynamic history that would unfold in the centuries to come.

As we conclude this chapter on medieval Cyprus and the era of Crusader rule, it becomes evident that the island's history is a testament to its remarkable adaptability, evolution, and resilience in the face of historical challenges. The medieval period, characterised by Crusader dominion and the fusion of diverse cultures, has left an enduring legacy on Cyprus's identity.

Throughout the medieval era, Cyprus showcased its capacity to adapt to changing circumstances. The island witnessed significant political shifts, cultural synthesis, and the construction of impressive architectural landmarks, all of which reflected its ability to evolve in response to external influences.

The medieval period served as a foundational chapter in Cyprus's history, laying the groundwork for the dynamic and unbridled centuries that followed. The interplay of Crusader dominion and cultural synthesis during this era shaped the island's unique identity, which would continue to evolve in response to the inexorable forces of history.

Cyprus's history is not only about external influences but also about the enduring resilience of its people. The Cypriots actively participated in shaping their island's destiny, navigating the complexities of Crusader rule and cultural fusion, and contributing to the island's rich heritage. Medieval Cyprus and the era of Crusader rule represent a pivotal and dynamic chapter in the island's history. It showcases Cyprus's adaptability, its ability to synthesise diverse cultural influences, and the enduring resilience of its people. This chapter set the stage for the island's future, shaping its identity and history as it continued its journey through time, marked by both challenges and triumphs.

Richard the Lionheart: As previously mentioned, Richard the Lionheart played a pivotal role in the history of medieval Cyprus. His conquest of the island in 1191 A.D. marked the beginning of Crusader rule, introducing Western European influences to Cyprus.

Lusignan Monarchs: The Lusignan dynasty, originally from France, ruled Cyprus during this era. Notable figures from this dynasty include:

- **Guy de Lusignan**: He was the first Lusignan monarch to rule Cyprus and played a key role in shaping the island's cultural and political landscape.

- **Hugh IV**: Another prominent Lusignan ruler, his reign saw further developments in Cyprus's feudal system and the construction of medieval fortifications.

IMPORTANT PLACES:

Saint Nicholas Cathedral in Famagusta: This Gothic cathedral is a significant architectural marvel of medieval Cyprus, showcasing the influence of Western European design and craftsmanship on the island.

Hilarion Castle: Located in the Kyrenia Mountains, it is another remarkable example of medieval fortifications in Cyprus.

The Ottoman era, spanning from 1570 A.D. to 1878 A.D., reveals a captivating and multifaceted chapter in the history of Cyprus. This period is etched with the enduring influence of Ottoman rule, a complex mixture of cultural coexistence, and the island's strategic significance in the Eastern Mediterranean. It unfolds as a captivating narrative of transformation, adaptation, and the interplay of diverse cultures and historical forces.

OTTOMAN CONQUEST AND GOVERNANCE

The year 1570 A.D. marked a watershed moment in Cyprus's history as Ottoman rule was established following the siege of Famagusta. This event held profound and enduring consequences for the island, entailing its integration into the Ottoman Empire, administrative shifts, and the emergence of influential figures of power. Cyprus's narrative during this period exemplifies the transformative power of conquest and the lasting imprint of Ottoman governance in shaping the island's identity. It firmly established Ottoman dominance over the island, ushering in significant changes across its political, social, and cultural landscapes.

Following the conquest, Cyprus seamlessly integrated into the vast expanse of the Ottoman Empire. The island assumed its role as one of the empire's provinces, contributing to the empire's expansive territorial reach.

The Ottomans introduced a novel administrative system to govern Cyprus, replacing previous structures. Ottoman officials known as pashas assumed responsibilities for overseeing the island's administration. These changes brought about alterations in governance and taxation, reflecting the island's alignment with Ottoman norms.

Under Ottoman rule, Cyprus's inhabitants became subjects of the Ottoman sultan, bound by Ottoman laws and regulations. The island's legal and social framework underwent transformation to conform to Ottoman standards.

Notably, during this period, a prominent figure emerged in Cyprus's history, namely Lala Mustafa Pasha. His leadership and military prowess played a pivotal role in the successful siege of Famagusta, a momentous event in the overall conquest of the island.

Lala Mustafa Pasha

The Ottoman era in Cyprus unfolded as a unique chapter, characterised by a rich flourish of religious and cultural coexistence. This period bore witness to the convergence of various traditions, architectural legacies, and a flourishing of both Christian and Muslim practices.

Despite Ottoman rule, Greek Orthodox Christianity remained a foundational facet of Cypriot identity. Churches and monasteries continued to flourish, serving as spiritual and communal hubs for the island's Christian population. These religious institutions diligently preserved Byzantine traditions, contributing significantly to the preservation of Cypriot heritage.

The Ottoman authorities left an indelible architectural legacy on the island. They erected mosques, which not only served as centres for Muslim worship but also as arenas for cultural expression. Madrasas, or educational institutions, provided platforms for religious and academic learning. Public baths, known as hamams, became integral to hygiene and social gatherings, exemplifying Ottoman influence in daily life.

The historic city of Nicosia, encircled by well-preserved Venetian walls, metamorphosed into a vibrant symbol of cultural coexistence. Inhabitants, both Christian and Muslim, shared the same urban space, creating a unique blend of traditions and practices. The city thrived as a hub for commerce, education, and artistic exchange, fostering a cosmopolitan atmosphere that enriched Cyprus's multifaceted identity.

Hala Sultan Mosque in Larnaca

This cultural amalgamation engendered a rich mosaic of traditions, crafts, and cuisine. Cypriot culture absorbed influences from both Greek and Turkish traditions, giving rise to a distinctive fusion of culinary delights, artistic expressions, and craftsmanship. This fusion persists in shaping Cyprus's identity, with culinary delights like halloumi cheese and traditions like Lefkaritika lacework attesting to this rich heritage.

Venetian Walls Nicosia

The Ottoman era in Cyprus was distinguished by the harmonious blend of religious and cultural coexistence. While Greek Orthodox Christianity remained central to Cypriot identity, Ottoman architecture, Islamic traditions, and the vibrant melting pot of Nicosia contributed to a multifaceted cultural mosaic that continues to shape the island's identity today. This era stands as a testament to the resilience and adaptability of Cyprus's diverse communities and the enduring legacy of their interactions.

Cyprus's prosperity during the Ottoman era found its roots in its fertile lands and strategic location, which played pivotal roles in the island's economic growth and regional prominence. Nevertheless, this period was not without its challenges, reflecting the intricate dynamics between the local populace and Ottoman authorities, as well as external threats.

Cyprus's fertile soils and favourable climate facilitated the cultivation of diverse crops, including citrus fruits, cotton, tobacco, and high-quality silk production. These agricultural pursuits significantly contributed to the island's economic expansion and affluence.

Cyprus blossomed as a thriving centre for trade, serving as a vital link between the Ottoman Empire and the broader Mediterranean world. Its strategic location eased the movement of goods and people, rendering it an indispensable node in the Ottoman trade network.

Despite economic prosperity, this period bore witness to periodic uprisings and revolts on the island, reflecting the intricate relationship between the local population and Ottoman authorities, as well as occasional discontent among the inhabitants. These uprisings underscored the challenges of governing a diverse and culturally rich island like Cyprus.

Cyprus encountered external threats during the Ottoman era, including assaults by pirates and rival powers. The Mediterranean was a volatile region, and the island's strategic location rendered it vulnerable to such challenges. Safeguarding its coastlines and preserving security emerged as perpetual concerns for both local and Ottoman authorities.

Cyprus's economic prosperity during the Ottoman era was a consequence of its fertile lands and strategic positioning, fostering agricultural and trade activities. Nonetheless, this period also witnessed periodic uprisings, reflecting the intricate dynamics between the local populace and Ottoman rulers, as well as external threats that necessitated vigilance and security measures. Cyprus's narrative during this era is a testament to the island's resilience and capacity to navigate both opportunities and challenges in a dynamic Mediterranean context.

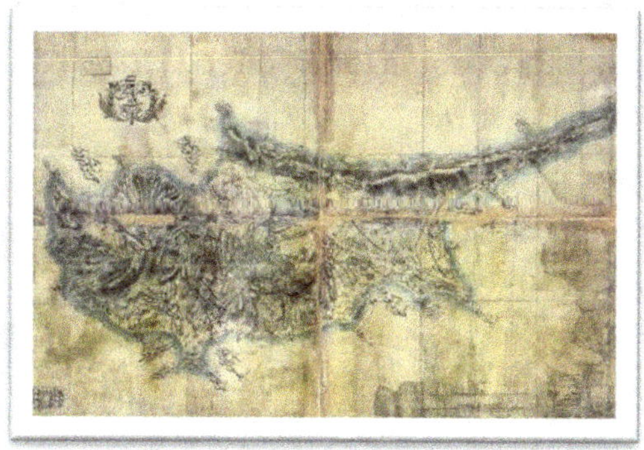

Ottoman Cyprus in 1873

Lala Mustafa Pasha: As previously mentioned, Lala Mustafa Pasha played a crucial role in the Ottoman conquest of Cyprus in 1570. His military leadership and strategic acumen were instrumental in the successful siege of Famagusta.

Ottoman Pashas of Cyprus: Various Ottoman governors or pashas ruled over Cyprus during this period, each contributing to the island's governance and administration. These officials held significant authority in Cyprus, overseeing the island's affairs on behalf of the Ottoman Empire.

IMPORTANT PLACES:

Famagusta: Famagusta, also known as Gazimağusa, was a pivotal city in the history of Cyprus during the Ottoman era. It was the site of a protracted siege and conquest by the Ottomans in 1570-1571. Famagusta's significance in this historical context cannot be overstated.

Nicosia: The capital city of Cyprus, Nicosia, played a central role in the island's Ottoman history. The city's cosmopolitan atmosphere, with its blending of diverse cultures, exemplified the coexistence of Christians and Muslims during this era.

Mosques and Madrasas: The Ottoman era in Cyprus witnessed the construction of numerous mosques and madrasas (educational institutions). These places of worship and learning served as integral parts of Cypriot life and architectural heritage, reflecting Ottoman cultural influence.

Venetian Walls of Nicosia: The well-preserved Venetian walls that encircle the old city of Nicosia are not only significant for their historical value but also symbolize the endurance of past architectural legacies amidst Ottoman rule.

Cyprus's Agricultural Land: Cyprus's fertile agricultural lands were crucial for the island's economic prosperity during the Ottoman era. These lands were vital for the cultivation of crops and the island's contribution to Ottoman agricultural production.

Cyprus's Coastal Fortifications: Due to the island's strategic location, coastal fortifications and defences were essential. These fortifications aimed to safeguard against external threats, including piracy and rival powers in the Mediterranean.

The colonial era of Cyprus, spanning from 1878 A.D. to 1960 A.D., unfolds as a period of profound transformation, political upheaval, and the island's transition from Ottoman rule to British administration. This chapter delves into the intricate fabric of British colonialism and its lasting impact on Cyprus.

THE BRITISH ARRIVAL

In the year 1878, a pivotal event unfolded, casting a profound and enduring influence over the island of Cyprus. At that juncture, the mighty Ottoman Empire, strategically during the Russo-Turkish War, made the momentous decision to cede control of Cyprus to the British Empire. This transfer of power marked the commencement of British colonial rule, an era that would span over eight decades, significantly shaping Cyprus's historical narrative.

With the advent of British administration, a new order of governance took root, accompanied by a plethora of legal systems and infrastructure development. These transformative changes played a pivotal role in shaping Cyprus's destiny. Sir Garnet Wolseley, a distinguished figure of the time, assumed the role of the first British High

Commissioner for Cyprus. In this capacity, he presided over the initial phases of British rule, laying the groundwork for the governance and policies that would define this colonial period.

Sir Garnet Wolseley

Under British rule, Cyprus underwent substantial modernisation and transformation. The British administration introduced administrative reforms and modernised the legal system, leaving an indelible mark on the island's institutions. The legal framework established during this era became a cornerstone for Cyprus's modern legal system.

Furthermore, the British oversaw significant infrastructure development that enhanced the island's connectivity and functionality. Roads, ports, and other essential facilities were constructed, facilitating trade and communication. These developments not only spurred economic growth but also improved the interconnectedness of Cyprus's regions.

Over the eight decades of British colonial rule, Cyprus became a melting pot of cultures and influences. The coexistence of British colonial authorities with the diverse local population, including Greek and Turkish communities, added complexity to Cyprus's social fabric. This period laid the groundwork for the intricate intercommunal dynamics that would continue to shape the island's history.

The cession of Cyprus to the British Empire in 1878 marked the inception of a transformative chapter in the island's history. The era of British colonial rule ushered in profound changes in governance, legal systems, and infrastructure development. Sir Garnet Wolseley played instrumental roles in shaping the early stages of British administration. This period of colonial rule set the stage for subsequent historical developments in Cyprus and left an enduring legacy that continues to influence the island's identity and trajectory.

Hoisting the British Flag in Nicosia (1878)

During the period of British colonial rule in Cyprus, which spanned over eight decades, the island underwent significant transformations across various facets of its society and governance. These changes left an indelible mark on Cyprus's history and shaped its modern identity.

One of the most notable aspects of British administration was the substantial administrative reforms implemented. The British sought to modernise the island's legal system, introducing new laws and institutions that reflected contemporary British legal principles. This modernisation of the legal framework had a far-reaching impact, providing Cyprus with a more structured and efficient legal system that would endure long after British rule had ended.

Education also received attention during this period, with concerted efforts made to expand educational institutions. Schools were established and improved, contributing to the growth of literacy and education on the island. This investment in education laid the foundation for a more knowledgeable and skilled population in the years to come.

The capital city of Nicosia underwent significant urban development under British rule. This development included the introduction of modern infrastructure, such as railways and roads, which improved transportation and connectivity, facilitating trade and economic growth. These developments not only enhanced the overall quality of life for the residents of Nicosia but also further connected the various regions of Cyprus.

Culturally, Cyprus experienced the influence of British traditions and institutions. The English language gained prominence, becoming a lingua franca for communication and commerce. British-style governance, with its emphasis on bureaucracy and administrative structures, left a lasting imprint on Cyprus's political landscape.

The island's population during this time was diverse, consisting of Greek Cypriots, Turkish Cypriots, and British expatriates. While these communities coexisted, it was not without occasional tensions and disparities. The complex interplay between these groups contributed to the evolving dynamics of Cyprus's social fabric and would become a significant factor in the island's future political developments.

British colonial rule brought about a period of substantial change and development in Cyprus. Administrative reforms, legal modernisation, educational expansion, and urban development transformed the island. Culturally, British influences were evident, impacting language, governance, and institutions. The coexistence of diverse communities added complexity to the social landscape, setting the stage for the intricate intercommunal dynamics that would continue to shape Cyprus's history.

The 20th century had a profound impact on the island of Cyprus, with the two World Wars playing pivotal roles in shaping its history. These events brought about significant political, social, and economic changes that would have far-reaching consequences.

During World War I, Cyprus assumed strategic importance as a base for British military operations in the Eastern Mediterranean. Figures like General Sir George Milne played instrumental roles in the defence of the island during this conflict. Cyprus became a vital hub for British forces, facilitating their operations in the region.

As World War II unfolded, Cyprus once again found itself in a precarious position. The looming threat of Axis occupation cast a shadow over the island, leading to substantial social and economic disruptions. The fear of invasion and occupation intensified the challenges faced by the Cypriot population during this period.

The British Army in Cyprus (1941)

RAAF Hurricane Cyprus 1942

In the post-war era, political unrest began to simmer on the island. Greek Cypriots, inspired by global movements for independence from colonial rule, started demanding greater political rights and autonomy. Their ultimate aspiration was "enosis," the union of Cyprus with Greece. This movement gained momentum, reflecting the desire of Greek Cypriots for self-determination.

In parallel, Turkish Cypriots, cognisant of their minority status within an overwhelmingly Greek Cypriot population, expressed concerns about their own rights and interests. They were apprehensive about the prospect of "enosis," as it could potentially marginalise their community. Prominent leaders emerged on both sides of this divide to champion their respective causes.

Archbishop Makarios III emerged as a key leader representing the Greek Cypriot community. He became a prominent advocate for enosis and played a pivotal role in shaping the political landscape of Cyprus during this period. On the Turkish Cypriot side, Dr. Fazıl Küçük emerged as a prominent figure, advocating for the rights and interests of the Turkish Cypriot minority.

These political and social tensions, exacerbated by the complex history and demographics of the island, set the stage for the intricate intercommunal dynamics that would define Cyprus's history in the years to come. The struggle for Cyprus's future direction, encompassing questions of identity, independence, and communal rights, would continue to shape the island's trajectory throughout the latter half of the 20th century.

Archbishop Makarios III

The mid-20th century brought mounting tensions to Cyprus, ultimately leading the island on a path towards independence. During the 1950s, nationalist movements gained significant momentum on both sides of the ethnic divide that had long characterised the island.

As these tensions escalated, a significant turning point came in 1960 with the signing of the Zürich-London Agreements These agreements laid the groundwork for the establishment of the Republic of Cyprus, marking a crucial step towards independence. The Republic of Cyprus was envisioned as an independent nation, and it was designed to have a power-sharing arrangement between the Greek Cypriot and Turkish Cypriot communities.

Under this arrangement, Cyprus was intended to be a bi-communal state, with provisions for the participation of both Greek and Turkish Cypriots in the government. The aim was to create a harmonious coexistence between the two communities within a single nation.

However, it's worth noting that even as Cyprus achieved independence, the Zürich-London Agreements stipulated that the British would retain sovereignty over military bases on the island. These bases continued to play a strategic role in British military operations in the Eastern Mediterranean.

The establishment of the Republic of Cyprus was seen as a potential solution to the longstanding tensions on the island, but the complex intercommunal dynamics and external geopolitical factors would continue to challenge the fragile balance of power in Cyprus. These dynamics would ultimately lead to further complications and conflicts in the years that followed, shaping the course of Cyprus's modern history.

CONCLUSION

The colonial era in Cyprus represented a significant and transformative period in the island's history. It marked a critical transition from Ottoman rule to British administration, bringing with it a multitude of changes and challenges that would leave a lasting legacy.

The legacy of this colonial era is profound and enduring. It not only set the stage for the complex and often unrestrained modern history of Cyprus but also left indelible marks on its cultural, political, and social landscape. The interplay of British influences, the coexistence of diverse communities, and the demands for political rights during this period laid the foundation for the intricate dynamics that continue to define Cyprus today.

Sir Garnet Wolseley: As mentioned earlier, Sir Garnet Wolseley was the first British High Commissioner for Cyprus and played a pivotal role in shaping the early phases of British colonial rule on the island.

General Sir George Milne: During World War I, General Sir George Milne was a prominent figure in Cyprus, overseeing its role as a strategic base for British military operations in the Eastern Mediterranean.

Archbishop Makarios III: Archbishop Makarios III emerged as a key leader representing the Greek Cypriot community in the mid-20th century. He played a crucial role in advocating for the Greek Cypriot cause and was a central figure in the struggle for Cyprus's independence.

Dr. Fazıl Küçük: Dr. Fazıl Küçük was a prominent leader on the Turkish Cypriot side, advocating for the rights and interests of the Turkish Cypriot minority. He played a significant role in shaping the political landscape of Cyprus during this period.

IMPORTANT PLACES:

Nicosia: The capital city of Cyprus, Nicosia, played a central role in the island's colonial history. It underwent significant urban development and transformation under British rule. Nicosia continues to be a focal point for political and cultural activities on the island.

British Military Bases: The British retained sovereignty over military bases on Cyprus even after the island achieved independence. These bases played a strategic role in British military operations in the Eastern Mediterranean and are still in operation today.

Cyprus's Educational Institutions: During the colonial era, educational institutions were expanded and improved across the island. These schools and colleges played a vital role in shaping the education and intellectual landscape of Cyprus.

Cyprus's Infrastructure: British colonial rule brought about the development of crucial infrastructure, including roads, ports, and railways. These infrastructure projects not only facilitated trade and economic growth but also enhanced connectivity within the island.

These influential figures and important places collectively contributed to the complex and multifaceted history of Cyprus during the colonial era. They left lasting imprints on the island's political, social, and cultural development, shaping its trajectory in the 20th century and beyond.

CHAPTER 7: CONFLICT AND INDEPENDENCE (1955 A.D. - 1960 A.D.)

The period from 1955 A.D. to 1960 A.D. in Cyprus's history was a chapter defined by a complex interplay of events, negotiations, and conflicts that would chart the island's path towards independence. In this chapter, we delve deeply into the arduous struggle for sovereignty and the myriad challenges confronted during this pivotal era.

During this period, Cyprus bore witness to a fervent and often turbulent pursuit of self-determination. The desire for sovereignty and independence burned passionately within the Cypriot population, but achieving these aspirations was far from straightforward.

Central to this era was the struggle between Greek Cypriots, who yearned for Cyprus to unite with Greece in a concept known as "enosis," and Turkish Cypriots, who were understandably concerned about their minority status within a predominantly Greek Cypriot population. This ethno-political divide added layers of complexity to the quest for independence and sovereignty.

Diplomacy and negotiations played a pivotal role in this period. Achieving a harmonious coexistence between the two communities within a single nation was a formidable challenge. The enduring legacy of colonial rule, coupled with deep-seated historical and cultural differences, created tensions that would persist long after independence was achieved.

The struggle for sovereignty and the intricate negotiations during this era set the stage for the complex and often contentious modern history of Cyprus. The challenges faced and the compromises made during this period continue to influence the island's political landscape and social dynamics to this day.

EMERGENCE OF EOKA AND THE DEMAND FOR ENOSIS

The mid-20th century marked a pivotal period in Cyprus's history with the emergence of the National Organisation of Cypriot Fighters (EOKA), a Greek Cypriot nationalist organisation led by the charismatic and influential figure, George Grivas. EOKA's mission was clear: to achieve the unification of Cyprus with Greece, or "enosis." However, this pursuit led to a relentless guerrilla campaign against British colonial rule, creating a climate of tension and instability on the island.

The Flag of EOKA

Georgios Grivas 1976

Yet, this era of unrest was not without complications. The conflict between EOKA and British authorities sometimes spilled over into violent clashes with Turkish Cypriot communities. The ethno-political divide on the island, coupled with the pursuit of enosis, exacerbated tensions and created a challenging environment.

Key figures in this period were George Grivas and Archbishop Makarios III. Grivas, as the leader of EOKA, was the driving force behind the nationalist movement, while Archbishop Makarios III lent his moral and political authority to the cause. Their leadership galvanised Greek Cypriot support for enosis.

This period, marked by EOKA's activities, was characterised by palpable instability and unrest. The struggle for enosis, violent confrontations with British forces, and tensions within the Cypriot community itself left an indelible mark on the island's history. This era set the stage for the complex and often contentious path towards Cyprus's eventual independence and its ongoing challenges related to intercommunal dynamics and national identity.

THE ZÜRICH-LONDON AGREEMENTS

In 1959, a significant diplomatic initiative unfolded in an earnest effort to address the escalating crisis in Cyprus. The Zürich-London Agreements aimed to provide a structured framework for the establishment of the Republic of Cyprus, an independent nation tasked with the challenging responsibility of navigating power-sharing between Greek and Turkish Cypriots.

The Zürich-London Agreements
From left to right: Greek Prime Minister Karamanlis, Turkish Minister of Foreign Affairs Zorlu and Turkish Prime Minister Menderes at the negotiations in Zürich, Switzerland

The Zurich-London Agreements were a pivotal moment in Cyprus's history, designed to outline a blueprint for a unified nation that could accommodate the interests of both Greek and Turkish Cypriot communities. One of their key features was the establishment of a power-sharing arrangement within the Republic of Cyprus to ensure meaningful representation for both communities.

To safeguard this delicate balance, the Zurich-London Agreements designated Britain, Greece, and Turkey as guarantor powers. These nations were entrusted with the responsibility of ensuring the provisions of the agreements were upheld and that the fragile equilibrium on the island was preserved.

The involvement of guarantor powers underscored the international dimension of the Cyprus issue and the recognition of its significance beyond the island's borders. It reflected broader geopolitical considerations in the Eastern Mediterranean during this period.

The Zurich-London Agreements of 1959 marked a determined effort to address the crisis in Cyprus and lay the foundation for the Republic of Cyprus. These agreements set out a comprehensive plan for power-sharing and the establishment of an independent nation. The role of guarantor powers, Britain, Greece, and Turkey, was crucial in maintaining stability and ensuring the delicate balance between Greek and Turkish Cypriots. This diplomatic initiative marked a significant chapter in Cyprus's journey towards independence and set the stage for the complex intercommunal dynamics and international involvement that would continue to shape its history.

The journey towards independence for Cyprus was marked by formidable challenges, requiring a careful and precarious balance between the fervent aspirations of Greek Cypriots for enosis (unification with Greece) and the legitimate concerns of Turkish Cypriots about their minority status on the island.

Negotiations during this period were complex and contentious, with both sides advocating fiercely for their interests. The Greek Cypriots were determined to secure a future united with Greece, driven by deep historical and cultural roots. In contrast, Turkish Cypriots were acutely aware of their minority status and had genuine concerns about their rights, security, and political representation.

Dr. Fazıl Küçük played a pivotal role in representing the Turkish Cypriot community during these intricate negotiations. His leadership underscored the importance of the Turkish Cypriot voice in shaping the island's future.

Reconciling these competing interests and concerns was a painstaking process, involving not only Cypriots but also international stakeholders, as seen through the role of guarantor powers like Britain, Greece, and Turkey. The delicate balancing act aimed to find a solution that would guarantee the rights and security of both communities within an independent Cyprus.

Dr. Fazıl Küçük

The road to independence for Cyprus was fraught with monumental challenges, chiefly the need to reconcile the passionate aspirations of Greek Cypriots for enosis with the valid concerns of Turkish Cypriots about their minority status. Negotiations during this period were complex and contentious, with both sides fiercely advocating for their interests. Dr. Fazıl Küçük played crucial roles in representing the Turkish Cypriot community. The eventual success in establishing the Republic of Cyprus hinged on finding a careful balance that could protect the rights and interests of both communities in the newly independent nation.

INDEPENDENCE AND THE BI-COMMUNAL CONSTITUTION

A momentous and historic date in Cyprus's history occurred on August 16, 1960, when the island achieved its long-sought-after independence. This marked the official establishment of the Republic of Cyprus, signifying a new chapter in the nation's history.

Archbishop Makarios III, a towering figure in the enosis movement and a symbol of Greek Cypriot aspirations, ascended to the presidency of the newly independent Cyprus. His election to this prominent position was a testament to his leadership and the hopes of the Greek Cypriot community for a united and sovereign Cyprus.

In the same vein, Dr. Fazıl Küçük represented the Turkish Cypriot community during negotiations, assumed the role of Vice President. His appointment was significant in recognising the importance of Turkish Cypriot participation in the governance of the newly formed Republic of Cyprus.

The government that took shape was bi-communal in nature, reflecting the diverse composition of Cyprus's population. This government bore the weighty responsibility of representing the interests of both Greek and Turkish Cypriots. The vision was to create a harmonious and inclusive future for the nation, where the rights and concerns of both communities would be safeguarded.

The establishment of the Republic of Cyprus was seen as a moment of optimism and promise, with the hope that it would provide a platform for peaceful coexistence and cooperation between Greek and Turkish Cypriots. However, as subsequent events would reveal, the challenges of maintaining this delicate balance and fostering true unity on the island were formidable.

In the years that followed, Cyprus's journey as an independent nation would be marked by complex intercommunal dynamics, external pressures, and political challenges. The vision of a harmonious future, symbolised by the bi-communal government of 1960, would face significant tests in the decades to come, shaping the island.

George Grivas: George Grivas, also known as "Dighenis," was a central figure in the mid-20th-century struggle for enosis. He led the National Organisation of Cypriot Fighters (EOKA) and played a pivotal role in the Greek Cypriot nationalist movement.

Archbishop Makarios III: Archbishop Makarios III was a prominent leader who symbolized Greek Cypriot aspirations for enosis. He became the first President of the Republic of Cyprus after independence and was a key figure in shaping the nation's early political landscape.

Dr. Fazıl Küçük: Dr. Fazıl Küçük was a respected leader representing the Turkish Cypriot community during negotiations for independence. He became the Vice President of the Republic of Cyprus, highlighting the importance of Turkish Cypriot participation in the government.

IMPORTANT PLACES:

Republic of Cyprus: The establishment of the Republic of Cyprus in 1960 was a historic moment, signifying the island's long-sought independence. The capital city, Nicosia, became the seat of the new government.

Bi-Communal Government: The bi-communal government of Cyprus, with its Greek Cypriot President (Archbishop Makarios III) and Turkish Cypriot Vice President (Dr. Fazıl Küçük), symbolised the hope for peaceful coexistence and cooperation between the two communities. It was a crucial institution in the early years of the Republic.

These influential figures and significant places played pivotal roles in shaping the complex and often turbulent period of Cyprus's struggle for independence and the establishment of the Republic of Cyprus. They represented the aspirations, concerns, and hopes of the island's diverse communities, and their actions and decisions continue to influence Cyprus's history and politics to this day.

The years between 1960 and 1974 in Cyprus's history were marked by disturbing and unsettling developments, leaving an indelible mark on the island's socio-political landscape. This chapter unravels the complex network of intercommunal strife, external interventions, and the profound shifts that defined Cyprus during this period.

Intercommunal tensions became a defining feature of this era. Despite initial hopes for peaceful coexistence, the relationship between the Greek and Turkish Cypriot communities deteriorated significantly. The power-sharing arrangements within the Republic of Cyprus, aimed at providing representation for both groups, faltered in the face of deep-rooted divisions, historical grievances, and conflicting interests.

External influences added layers of complexity. The involvement of external powers, particularly Greece and Turkey, injected new dimensions into the Cyprus issue. These nations were perceived as protectors of their respective ethnic communities on the island, amplifying the international dimension of the conflict.

The socio-political landscape underwent seismic changes. Political stalemate, ethnic violence, and pervasive mistrust became the norm, creating an atmosphere of instability and uncertainty. The dream of a unified and harmonious Cyprus seemed increasingly distant.

The years spanning from 1960 to 1974 were characterised by a painful narrative of struggle and strife. The Cyprus conflict during this era had profound and enduring consequences, shaping the island's political trajectory and social fabric for decades to come.

Now, we embark on a deeper exploration of the events and dynamics that unfolded during this period, delving into the intricacies of intercommunal conflict, external interventions, and the quest for a resolution to the Cyprus issue. This comprehensive examination will provide a more profound understanding of the complexities and challenges that shaped Cyprus during these turbulent years.

FRAGILE INDEPENDENCE AND ETHNIC TENSIONS

In 1960, the birth of the Republic of Cyprus represented a significant milestone, founded on the principles of power-sharing and cooperation between the Greek and Turkish Cypriot communities. However, the fragility of this arrangement became evident relatively quickly.

The core idea behind the Republic of Cyprus was to create a bi-communal state where both Greek and Turkish Cypriots could coexist harmoniously and share power. This vision was underpinned by ideals of inclusivity and unity.

Nevertheless, beneath the surface, tensions and challenges simmered. Mutual mistrust began to fester as both communities grappled with historical grievances, cultural differences, and competing interests. The weight of these unresolved issues strained the delicate balance that the Republic of Cyprus had sought to achieve.

The coexistence envisaged at independence seemed increasingly elusive as time passed. The power-sharing arrangements faced difficulties, and the promise of a unified and harmonious Cyprus began to wane. The fragility of the arrangement set the stage for the complex intercommunal tensions and conflicts that would come to define Cyprus's modern history.

In essence, the birth of the Republic of Cyprus in 1960 was a noble attempt to foster cooperation between Greek and Turkish Cypriots. However, the challenges of reconciling deeply rooted differences and historical grievances proved formidable, leading to a growing sense of mistrust and frustration that would ultimately have far-reaching consequences in the years that followed.

As the 1960s progressed, the political landscape of Cyprus underwent a troubling transformation, characterised by a growing polarisation between the Greek Cypriot and Turkish Cypriot communities. These divisions were rooted in long-standing grievances and concerns.

Greek Cypriots clung steadfastly to their dream of enosis, the unification of Cyprus with Greece, an aspiration that had endured for decades. This historical and cultural connection to Greece remained a powerful driving force within the Greek Cypriot community, and the desire for enosis remained a potent element of their political agenda.

Conversely, Turkish Cypriots were deeply apprehensive about their security and status within the Republic of Cyprus. Concerns about being a minority within the predominantly Greek Cypriot republic loomed large. This unease was heightened by historical memories of intercommunal conflicts and the uncertainties surrounding their place in the new nation.

As a result of these growing divisions and fears, the delicate bi-communal framework upon which the Republic of Cyprus had been founded began to crumble. The sparks of intercommunal violence began to fly, reflecting the heightened tensions and mistrust between the two communities. The political landscape became increasingly polarised, with both sides advocating for their respective interests and security.

The 1960s, therefore, marked a troubling period in Cyprus's history, where the initial vision of a unified and harmonious nation began to erode amid the growing rift between Greek Cypriots and Turkish Cypriots. These developments set the stage for the more profound conflicts and challenges that would define Cyprus's trajectory in the following decades.

EXTERNAL INFLUENCES AND MILITARY INTERVENTION

The escalation of intercommunal conflict in Cyprus, a relatively small island in the Eastern Mediterranean, inevitably drew the attention of external powers. In 1964, as violence and instability mounted, the United Nations took action by deploying a peacekeeping force to Cyprus, known as UNFICYP (United Nations Peacekeeping Force in Cyprus).

United Nations Peacekeeping Force in Cyprus

Regrettably, despite the presence of UNFICYP, tensions on the island continued to simmer, and the prospect of a peaceful resolution remained elusive. The involvement of external powers, notably Greece and Turkey, further complicated the situation.

Greece saw itself as the protector of the Greek Cypriot community and actively supported their aspirations for enosis, injecting a strong nationalist dimension into the conflict and exacerbating tensions.

Turkey, on the other hand, perceived itself as the protector of the Turkish Cypriot community. Turkish leaders expressed deep concern about the security and rights of Turkish Cypriots within the Republic of Cyprus, heightening the potential for external intervention.

In 1974, these external concerns and the deteriorating situation culminated in a dramatic turn of events. Turkey, citing the need to protect Turkish Cypriots, conducted a military intervention in Cyprus. This intervention resulted in a de facto division of the island into Greek Cypriot-controlled and Turkish Cypriot-controlled areas, a situation that persists to this day.

The external interventions in Cyprus, particularly Turkey's military action in 1974, had profound and lasting consequences. They fundamentally altered the island's political landscape, cementing its division and deepening the ethnic and political fault lines that had emerged over the years. The Cyprus conflict, with its intercommunal tensions and external dimensions, remained a complex and unresolved issue, casting a long shadow over the region's geopolitics.

CONCLUSION

The period from 1960 to 1974 in Cyprus's history was characterised by profound intercommunal conflict, external interventions, and a dramatic shift in the island's socio-political landscape. The initial optimism that accompanied the establishment of the Republic of Cyprus in 1960 gave way to growing divisions, mistrust, and violence.

Despite noble efforts to create a bi-communal state where Greek and Turkish Cypriots could coexist harmoniously, the complexities of historical grievances, cultural differences, and competing interests proved insurmountable. The erosion of the bi-communal framework and the intensification of ethnic tensions set the stage for external interventions and military conflict.

The involvement of external powers, Greece and Turkey, injected a strong nationalist dimension into the conflict and further complicated the situation. The military intervention by Turkey in 1974 resulted in a de facto division of the island, a situation that persists to this day.

The period from 1960 to 1974 marked a riotous and painful chapter in Cyprus's history, with enduring consequences that continue to shape the island's political trajectory and social fabric. The Cyprus conflict, with its intercommunal tensions and external dimensions, remained an ongoing and complex issue in the region, casting a long shadow over the Eastern Mediterranean. In the subsequent chapters, we will delve deeper into the aftermath of the 1974 conflict and the continuing quest for a resolution to the Cyprus issue, exploring the complexities and challenges that have defined the island's modern history.

Archbishop Makarios III: Archbishop Makarios III, the first President of the Republic of Cyprus, continued to be a prominent figure during this period. He represented Greek Cypriot aspirations and played a key role in navigating the complex intercommunal tensions.

Dr. Fazıl Küçük: Dr. Fazıl Küçük, who had served as Vice President of the Republic of Cyprus, remained an influential figure representing Turkish Cypriot interests and concerns during this turbulent era.

George Grivas: While George Grivas's prominence had waned since the 1960s, his role as the leader of EOKA and his influence on Greek Cypriot nationalism continued to resonate during the period.

Nicosia: The capital city of Cyprus, Nicosia, remained a focal point for political and social developments during this period. It was divided into Greek Cypriot and Turkish Cypriot sectors after the 1974 conflict, symbolising the island's division.

Buffer Zone: After the Turkish military intervention in 1974, a buffer zone was established by the United Nations, dividing the island into areas controlled by Greek Cypriots and Turkish Cypriots. This buffer zone, also known as the Green Line, became a significant geographical feature and a symbol of the island's division.

These influential figures and important places played crucial roles in shaping the complex and turbulent period of Cyprus's history from 1960 to 1974. Their actions and decisions reflected the aspirations, concerns, and political dynamics of the Greek Cypriot and Turkish Cypriot communities, as well as the international dimension of the Cyprus conflict. These complexities continue to influence the island's politics and ongoing efforts to resolve the Cyprus issue.

The history of Cyprus from 1974 to the present day is a tale of division, conflict, diplomatic endeavours, and the enduring pursuit of reunification. In this chapter, we navigate the intricate array of events and complexities that have defined this turbulent era.

A DEFINING MOMENT: THE TURKISH INVASION OF 1974

1974 marked a pivotal juncture in Cyprus's history when the Turkish invasion reshaped the island dramatically. This military operation resulted in the de facto division of Cyprus into two distinct regions. In the north, control fell into the hands of the Turkish Cypriots, while the south remained predominantly under Greek Cypriot authority.

The division was solidified by the creation of the Green Line, a demarcation that physically separated the two sides. This line, marked with barriers and checkpoints, has been continuously patrolled and maintained by United Nations peacekeeping forces, who have played a pivotal role in preventing further conflict and preserving stability in the region.

The Green Line (Buffer Zone) Nicosia, Cyprus

DISPLACEMENT AND HUMANITARIAN CONSEQUENCES

The events of 1974 triggered a significant upheaval, leading to the forced displacement of populations. Greek Cypriots in the north and Turkish Cypriots in the south were abruptly uprooted from their homes, setting the stage for a multifaceted and enduring issue concerning property rights and restitution.

In the aftermath of the conflict, countless individuals and families found themselves separated from their ancestral homes and possessions. Greek Cypriots in the north were forced to abandon their residences and belongings, while Turkish Cypriots in the south faced similar upheaval. This mass migration left a poignant legacy of lost homes, cherished belongings, and the profound emotional toll of severed ties.

The question of property rights and restitution has remained at the forefront of the Cyprus problem. Displaced individuals on both sides of the divide have sought resolution and compensation for the losses they endured during this period. These efforts have entailed intricate negotiations and legal processes as individuals and their descendants seek to reclaim or receive compensation for their properties.

POLITICAL DIVISION AND DEEPENING STRIFE

The political division of Cyprus following the events of 1974 exacerbated existing ethnic and political fault lines. Greek Cypriots and Turkish Cypriots suddenly found themselves residing in separate regions, each under its own governance. This division not only physically separated the two communities but also deepened mutual distrust and suspicions, further complicating the already challenging path to reunification.

Before the division, Cyprus had a shared history, with Greek Cypriots and Turkish Cypriots coexisting on the island.

However, the establishment of separate governments in the south and north not only cemented a political divide but also created physical barriers that hindered interaction between the two communities. This separation fostered an atmosphere of mistrust as each side began to perceive the other with increasing suspicion.

The deepening ethnic and political divisions also had profound social and cultural implications. Communities that had once lived side by side and shared common traditions, customs, and even friendships were now estranged, as the separation reinforced notions of 'us' versus 'them.'

The pursuit of reunification in such a fraught environment became an arduous task. Diplomatic efforts, negotiations, and peace initiatives aimed at bridging the gap between Greek Cypriots and Turkish Cypriots faced significant obstacles due to the entrenched divisions. Issues such as governance structures, security arrangements, and property rights became contentious points of contention, making it challenging to reach a consensus that could lead to a comprehensive settlement.

FOREIGN INVOLVEMENT AND THE MILITARY PRESENCE

Another pivotal aspect of Cyprus's modern history has been the presence of foreign troops on the island. Following the Turkish invasion of 1974, Turkish military forces assumed control over the northern part of Cyprus, contributing to the de facto division of the island. This presence of foreign troops has remained a contentious issue and a significant impediment to achieving a comprehensive solution to the Cyprus problem.

In response to the Turkish invasion, the United Nations deployed peacekeeping forces to the island to help maintain stability and prevent further conflict. These UN forces have been stationed along the Green Line, serving as a buffer between the two sides. Their presence has played a crucial role in preventing the resumption of hostilities and facilitating humanitarian efforts.

Additionally, Cyprus's divided status and geopolitical significance have attracted the interest of various external actors, including Greece, Turkey, and international powers. These countries have played a role in shaping the dynamics of the Cyprus problem and have often been involved in diplomatic initiatives aimed at finding a solution.

The presence of foreign troops on the island, particularly the continued presence of Turkish military forces in the north, remains a deeply contentious issue. It has been a point of contention in peace negotiations and a source of tension between the parties involved. Achieving a resolution that addresses the security concerns of all parties while also ensuring the sovereignty and territorial integrity of Cyprus has proven to be a challenging task.

Despite the numerous challenges and obstacles, the pursuit of reunification has remained a central objective in Cyprus's modern history. Diplomatic initiatives, often facilitated by the United Nations, have sought to bring the Greek Cypriot and Turkish Cypriot communities together to negotiate a comprehensive settlement that would reunify the island.

These diplomatic efforts have involved numerous rounds of negotiations, summits, and peace talks. They have tackled a range of complex issues, including governance structures, power-sharing arrangements, property rights, and security guarantees. While there have been moments of optimism and progress in these negotiations, they have also been marked by periods of frustration and deadlock.

One significant milestone in the quest for reunification was the Annan Plan, put forward by then-UN Secretary-General Kofi Annan in 2004. The plan proposed a comprehensive settlement that included a federal system of government with power-sharing mechanisms and addressed the issues of property rights and the presence of foreign troops. However, in a referendum held in April 2004, the plan was rejected by the Greek Cypriot community, while it was accepted by the Turkish Cypriot community. This outcome underscored the deep divisions and complexities of the Cyprus problem.

Subsequent negotiations and initiatives have continued to grapple with the same fundamental challenges. The pursuit of a balanced and mutually acceptable solution remains a formidable task, with both sides holding firm to their respective positions and interests.

In recent years, there have been renewed efforts to restart negotiations and find a path towards reunification. These efforts have been met with cautious optimism, but the road ahead remains uncertain and challenging. The international community, including the United Nations, continues to play a role in facilitating dialogue and encouraging progress.

The quest for reunification in Cyprus remains a complex and ongoing process. Diplomatic initiatives have sought to bridge the divides between the Greek Cypriot and Turkish Cypriot communities, but achieving a comprehensive settlement that addresses the myriad of issues involved remains a formidable challenge.

CONCLUSION

The modern history of Cyprus from 1974 to the present has been characterised by division, conflict, diplomatic efforts, and the ongoing pursuit of reunification. The Turkish invasion of 1974 and the subsequent de facto division of the island have left a lasting legacy, with the Green Line serving as a stark reminder of the events of that period.

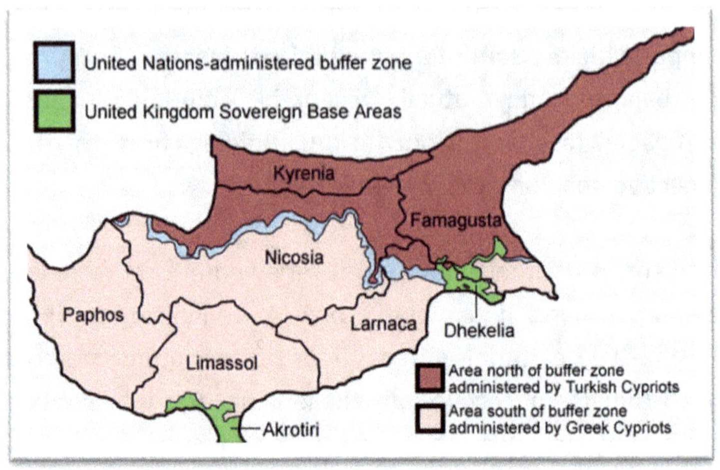

Turkish Republic of Northern Cyprus (TRNC) Boundaries

The displacement of populations, issues related to property rights and restitution, and the deepening of political and ethnic divisions have further complicated the path to reunification. The presence of foreign troops on the island and the involvement of external actors have added layers of complexity to the Cyprus problem.

Despite these challenges, the quest for reunification has persisted through diplomatic initiatives and negotiations. While there have been moments of optimism and progress, reaching a comprehensive settlement that satisfies the interests and concerns of both the Greek Cypriot and Turkish Cypriot communities remains a formidable task.

The modern history of Cyprus serves as a testament to the enduring complexities of the Cyprus problem and the deep-seated aspirations of many for a peaceful and reunified island. The future of Cyprus remains uncertain, but the desire for a resolution that addresses the grievances of all parties and paves the way for a more harmonious and prosperous future remains undiminished.

INFLUENTIAL FIGURES:

Rauf Denktaş: Rauf Denktaş was a key figure in the Turkish Cypriot community and played a prominent role in advocating for their interests during and after the events of 1974. He served as the first President of the self-declared Turkish Republic of Northern Cyprus (TRNC).

Glafcos Clerides: Glafcos Clerides was a significant Greek Cypriot political figure who served as President of the Republic of Cyprus from 1993 to 2003. He was involved in numerous negotiations and peace efforts aimed at resolving the Cyprus issue.

Kofi Annan: Kofi Annan, the former Secretary-General of the United Nations, played a pivotal role in the Cyprus peace process. He presented the Annan Plan in 2004, which was a comprehensive settlement proposal for the reunification of Cyprus.

Nicosia: Nicosia, the capital city of Cyprus, remains a crucial location for diplomatic negotiations and peace talks. The city is divided into Greek Cypriot and Turkish Cypriot sectors, and it has been the site of various meetings and discussions aimed at resolving the Cyprus problem.

Buffer Zone (Green Line): The Buffer Zone, also known as the Green Line, continues to be a significant geographical feature that divides the island. It serves as a symbol of the division and has checkpoints and United Nations patrols. It is an important location for peacekeeping efforts and negotiations.

United Nations Headquarters: The United Nations has been actively involved in facilitating peace talks and negotiations between the Greek Cypriot and Turkish Cypriot communities. The UN Headquarters in Cyprus, located in Nicosia, has been a central hub for diplomatic efforts to find a solution to the Cyprus problem.

These influential figures and important places have played crucial roles in shaping the events and dynamics of Cyprus from 1974 to the present day. They represent the key figures and locations associated with efforts to address the challenges and complexities of the Cyprus issue and the ongoing pursuit of reunification.

CHAPTER 10: CYPRUS IN THE FUTURE: A PREDICTIVE ACCOUNT

Ultimately, Cyprus's future hinges on the willingness of all involved parties to engage in dialogue, compromise, and reconciliation. Amid the uncertainties and complexities, the yearning for a peaceful, reunified, and prosperous Cyprus stands as a potent force that could guide the island towards a more harmonious and stable future.

As we look ahead to the future of Cyprus, it's important to recognise that the island's trajectory will be influenced by a range of factors and dynamics. While we can't predict specific individuals or places that will emerge as influential, we can identify some potential key developments and themes that may shape Cyprus in the coming decades:

LEADERSHIP TRANSITIONS:

Leadership changes on both sides of the divide in Cyprus could play a pivotal role in shaping the island's future. New leaders with fresh perspectives and approaches to the Cyprus problem may emerge, potentially creating opportunities for renewed dialogue and compromise.

Civil society organisations and grassroots movements can have a significant impact on the political landscape. They may advocate for reconciliation, peace, and reunification, exerting pressure on political leaders to take bold steps towards a comprehensive settlement.

INTERNATIONAL MEDIATORS:

The involvement of international mediators, such as the United Nations, may continue to be essential in facilitating negotiations between Greek Cypriots and Turkish Cypriots. Skilled diplomats and mediators can help bridge gaps and create an environment conducive to progress.

ENERGY INFRASTRUCTURE:

The development of energy infrastructure, including pipelines and export terminals, will be vital for harnessing Cyprus's energy resources. The construction of these facilities and associated partnerships with other countries will be significant for economic growth and regional stability.

Cyprus's location at the crossroads of Europe, Asia, and Africa places it at the forefront of migration and refugee challenges. Managing these issues, including asylum policies and cooperation with neighbouring countries, will be crucial.

The use of diplomatic channels and forums, such as international summits and multilateral organisations, can provide opportunities for Cyprus to engage with regional and global powers to address security and reunification concerns.

Cyprus may seek to diversify its economy beyond energy resources. Investments in technology, tourism, and education could be explored to reduce dependence on a single sector.

Encouraging cultural and educational exchanges between Greek Cypriots and Turkish Cypriots, as well as with international partners, can promote understanding and reconciliation at the grassroots level.

TOURISM AND HERITAGE PRESERVATION:

Tourism remains a vital industry for Cyprus. Balancing economic development with the preservation of cultural and historical heritage will be crucial for sustainable growth.

GREEN LINE AND BUFFER ZONE:

The management and potential transformation of the Green Line and Buffer Zone into areas of cooperation and reconciliation could be explored as part of reunification efforts.

CONCLUSION:

While we cannot predict specific influential figures or places in Cyprus's future, these potential developments and themes offer insights into the complex and multifaceted nature of the challenges and opportunities that lie ahead. The pursuit of reunification, economic growth, security, regional cooperation, and diplomacy will continue to be central to Cyprus's evolving narrative.

Name	Dates of Leadership
Archbishop Makarios III	1960 – 1977
Glafcos Clerides	1977 – 1988
George Vassiliou	1988 – 1993
Glafcos Clerides	1993 – 2003
Tassos Papadopoulos	2003 – 2008
Demetris Christofias	2008 - 2013
Nicos Anastasiades	2013 - 2023
Nikos Christodoulides	2023 – to date

Please note that the above list includes Presidents of the Republic of Cyprus, as Cyprus has a presidential system of government.

Nearchus (c. 360-300 B.C.) - An ancient Cypriot admiral and explorer who accompanied Alexander the Great on his campaign in Asia.

Zeno of Citium (c. 334-262 B.C.) - An ancient philosopher born in Cyprus and the founder of the Stoic school of philosophy.

George Grivas (1898-1974) - Leader of the National Organisation of Cypriot Fighters (EOKA), which fought for enosis (union with Greece) during the 1950s.

Dr. Fazıl Küçük (1906-1984) - A leader of the Turkish Cypriot community and Vice President of the Republic of Cyprus before the intercommunal conflict.

Archbishop Makarios III (1913-1977) - The first President of the Republic of Cyprus and a key figure in the island's struggle for independence.

Glafcos Clerides (1919-2013) - A prominent political figure who served as President of Cyprus and played a crucial role in the island's modern history.

Rauf Denktaş (1924-2012) - A significant Turkish Cypriot political figure who played a key role in the establishment of the Turkish Republic of Northern Cyprus.

Nikos Sampson (1935-2001) - Briefly served as the President of Cyprus in 1974 following the coup, before Turkish intervention led to his resignation.

Vassilis Michaelides (1930-2009) - A renowned Cypriot poet and writer known for his contributions to Cypriot literature.

Tassos Papadopoulos (1934-2008) - Cyprus's President from 2003 to 2008, known for his role in reunification efforts and his support for the Annan Plan.

Kypros Chrysostomides (1947-) - A Cypriot diplomat who served as the Chief Negotiator for the Accession of Cyprus to the European Union.

Demetris Christofias (1946-2019) - Cyprus's President from 2008 to 2013, who worked towards reunification and improved relations with Turkey.

Derviş Eroğlu (1938-) - A prominent Turkish Cypriot leader who served as President of the Turkish Republic of Northern Cyprus.

Makis Solomos (1953-) - A Cypriot composer and musician known for his contributions to modern Cypriot music.

Niki Marangou (1948-2020) - A Cypriot author and journalist known for her literary works and commentary on Cypriot society.

Andreas Vgenopoulos (1957-2016) - A Cypriot businessman and lawyer who played a significant role in the finance and legal sectors in Cyprus and Greece.

Tassos Papachristou (1965-) - A renowned Cypriot chef and restaurateur known for his contributions to the culinary scene on the island.

Eleni Theocharous (1953-) - A Cypriot politician and former Member of the European Parliament, actively involved in Cyprus's political landscape.

Costas Montis (1929-2004) - A celebrated Cypriot poet, playwright, and translator known for his influential works in the field of Cypriot literature.

Mehmet Ali Talat (1952-) - A prominent Turkish Cypriot politician who served as the President of the Turkish Republic of Northern Cyprus and advocated for a resolution to the Cyprus dispute through negotiations.

This diverse list represents individuals from various fields and eras, showcasing the rich history and contributions of Cypriots to the world.

INDEX

IMAGE CREDITS

Title	Citation
Cyprus Coat of Arms	Cyprus. (2023, September 11). In *Wikipedia*.
Cypriot Flag	Cyprus. (2023, September 11). In *Wikipedia*.
Cyprus's Location	bigstock-Mediterranean-Basin-Political-90186659-e1520759019145
Fossils Found in Aetokremnos in 1960	Aetokremnos. (2023, August 4). In *Wikipedia*.
Ancient City of Kition	JERRYE AND ROY KLOTZ MD, CC BY-SA 3.0 via Wikimedia Commons
Aphrodite	Illustrated by Engravings on Wood., Public domain, via Wikimedia Commons
Head of Aristotle	Sergey Sosnovskiy, CC BY-SA 2.0 via Wikimedia Commons
Bust of Plato	Tetraktys, CC BY-SA 3.0 via Wikimedia Commons
Roman Aqueduct in Nicosia	NicosiaSkylines, CC BY-SA 3.0 via Wikimedia Commons
The Site of Khirokitia	Khirokitia. (2023, July 10).
Alexander the Great (Mosaic)	Alexander the Great. (2023, September 3). In *Wikipedia*.
Emperor Nero and Senica	Seneca the Younger. (2023, September 1). In *Wikipedia*.
A Typical Byzantine Religious Icon	Anonymous icon painter, Public domain, via Wikimedia Commons
The Roman Empire	Roman Cyprus. (2023, April 7). In *Wikipedia*.
Constantine the Great	Constantine the Great. (2023, September 19). In *Wikipedia*.
Saint Barnabas	Barnabas. (2023, September 12). In *Wikipedia*.
Richard the Lionheart (King Richard I)	Richard I of England. (2023, September 19). In *Wikipedia*.
Guy de Lusignan	François-Édouard Picot, Public domain, via Wikimedia Commons
Kolossi Castle	Bukvoed, CC BY 4.0 via Wikimedia Commons
St. Hilarion Castle	Héctor Ochoa 'Robot8A', CC BY-SA 4.0 via Wikimedia Commons
St Nicholas Cathedral, Famagusta	A.Savin, FAL, via Wikimedia Commons
Lala Mustafa Pasha	Unidentified painter, public domain, via Wikimedia Commons
Hala Sultan Mosque, Larnaca	Dickelbers, CC BY-SA 3.0 via Wikimedia Commons
Venetian Walls Nicosia	NicosiaRepublicCyprus, CC BY-SA 3.0 via Wikimedia Commons
Ottoman Cyprus in 1873	Scanned image, public domain, via Wikimedia Commons
Sir Garnet Wolseley	Garnet Wolseley, 1st Viscount Wolseley. (2023, September 14). In *Wikipedia*
Hoisting the British Flag in Nicosia 1878	Illustrated London News, Public domain, via Wikimedia Commons
The British Army in Cyprus 1941	Davies L B (Lieut), Public domain, via Wikimedia Commons
RAAF Hurricane Cyprus 1942	Public domain, via Wikimedia Commons
The Flag of EOKA	Mikrobølgeovn, CC BY-SA 3.0, via Wikimedia Commons
Georgios Grivas 1976	CC0, via Wikimedia Commons
Archbishop Makarios III	Fernandez, Orlando, photographer., Public domain, via Wikimedia Commons
London and Zürich Agreements	London and Zürich Agreements. (2022, April 26). In *Wikipedia*.
Dr Fazıl Küçük	Fazıl Küçük. (2023, March 23). In *Wikipedia*.
United Nations Peacekeeping Force in Cyprus	United Nations Peacekeeping Force in Cyprus, Public domain, via Wikimedia Commons
The Green Line (Buffer Zone) Nicosia, Cyprus	Adam Jones from Kelowna, BC, Canada
Turkish Republic of Northern Cyprus (TRNC) Boundaries	https://creativecommons.org/licenses/by-sa/2.5>, via Wikimedia Commons

Martin Miller-Yianni, a London native born in 1958, hails from a humble working-class background. Although he initially pursued a career as a primary school teacher, his life took an unexpected turn when he ventured into Southeastern Europe in 2005. Martin's connection with the region is deeply personal; his father, a Greek Cypriot, tragically lost land and property when Turkey invaded Cyprus. Since his arrival, Martin has fully embraced the unique way of life and culture of Southeastern Europe, igniting a passion for writing within him. Having served as a journalist and researcher for a leading information website about this region, he has developed a profound knowledge, understanding, and first-hand experience of this part of the world. Martin's connection with Southeastern Europe, rooted in both personal and professional experiences, continues to inspire and influence his literary endeavours.

OTHER BOOKS BY THE AUTHOR

365 Bulgarian Adventures (2006)
Publication Pending

26 Tales of Humanities Trials (2023)
ISBN
978-619-92494-8-2

Simple Treasures in Bulgaria (2008)
ISBN
978-0-9559-8490-7

I'm Bad at Poems (2022)
ISBN
978-619-92494-2-0

Bulgaria Through the Ages (2023)
ISBN
978-1-4476-2777-7

Redemption of Love (2023)
ISBN
978-619-92494-0-6

100 Essential Recipes from Bulgaria (2011)
ISBN
978-1-4477-0260-3

Romania Through the Ages (2023)
ISBN
978-619-7742-19-0

www.ingramcontent.com/pod-product-compliance
Lightning Source LLC
LaVergne TN
LVHW050541200726
843506LV00001B/45